THE
SCULLERY
MAID

This is a work of fiction. All of the characters, events, and organizations portrayed in this work are either products of the authors' imagination or used fictitiously.

The Scullery Maid
Copyright © 2013 by Joseph Zettelmaier

All rights reserved. No part of this book may be reproduced in any form by any electronic or mechanical means including photocopying, recording, or information storage and retrieval without permission in writing from the author.

ISBN-13: 978-0692409442
ISBN-10: 0692409440

For information about production rights, visit:
www.jzettelmaier.com

Published by Sordelet Ink
Cover by David Blixt

THE SCULLERY MAID

A PLAY BY
JOSEPH ZETTELMAIER

Published by
Sordelet Ink

The Scullery Maid received its world premiere on Dec. 18, 2013, at the Jewish Ensemble Theatre in West Bloomfield, MI. It was directed by Joseph Albright. Set Design by Jennifer Maiseloff. Lighting Design by Neil Koivu. Costume Design by Mary Copenhagen. Props Design by Diane Ulseth. Sound Design by Matthew Lira. The production was stage managed by Harold Jurkiewicz, with Sharla Mills as assistant stage manager. The cast was as follows:

> BESS: Ruth Crawford
> DULCIE: Jacquie Floyd
> MIRIAM: Julia Garlotte
> PASCAL: Alan Madlane
> EDWARD III: John Manfredi

Cast of Characters

BESS, 50s, a cook
DULCIE, 20s-30s, a cook
MIRIAM, 20s, a cook
PASCAL, 60s-70s, a steward
EDWARD III, 47, King of England

Time

July, 1360

Place

The kitchen & royal bed chamber
of Nottingham Castle

ACT I

(In the darkness, the sound of a celebration. Music, revelers, etc... Lights rise on a kitchen in King Edward's castle. Two women work furiously to complete the final course-Royal Marchpane for desert. DULCIE is taking it out of the oven. BESS is preparing the icing)

BESS
Careful with that, girl! Girl!

DULCIE
Dulcie.

BESS
God help me, girl, if you drop it...

DULCIE
My name's Dulcie.

BESS
I'll put it on your grave marker if you drop that Marchpane!

(DULCIE sets it down on the table. She looks to BESS)

BESS
You just bought yourself another day of life.

(BESS bumps DULCIE out of the way & begins icing the pastry)

DULCIE
What's for me to do?

(She takes DULCIE's hand, and puts some icing on her finger)

BESS
Oily?

DULCIE
What?

BESS
Does it feel oily?

(DULCIE rubs it in her fingers)

DULCIE
Feels fine.

BESS
Not oily?

(Beat)

DULCIE
Dunno.

BESS
...useless as tits on a bull...Where's Miriam?

DULCIE
Dunno.

BESS
When did you see her last?

DULCIE
She gone out to pour wine.

BESS
That was twenty minutes ago!

DULCIE
Lots of cups to pour.

BESS
Give me the rose water.

(DULCIE looks, clueless as to what rose water looks like. She grabs a bowl and hands it to BESS. BESS is about to pour it into the bowl of icing, then stops)

BESS
What's this?

DULCE
...Ro-water?

BESS
Firstly, Rose Water. Secondly...

(She splashes some of the fluid into DULCIE's face)

BESS
Does that smell of roses?

DULCE
It stinks.

BESS
Aye, it stinks. Because it's damned soap water! If I'd poured this into the gilding, there'd be dukes

and barons turning their stomachs out! Christ! I'd swear you were a murderess if you had half the brains God gave a turnip!

(Beat. DULCIE stands there, on the verge of tears)

BESS
None of that now.

(DULCIE is losing the fight against her emotions)

BESS
I have no time for this. I have to get this dessert served for...

(DULCIE breaks down. BESS looks Heavenward)

BESS
Walk with me, Lord Jesus.

(She puts her arm around her, then moves DULCIE to a stool & seats her)

BESS
There we are, lamb. There we are.

DULCIE
I know I'm simple! But I try best I'm able!

BESS
Let's compose ourselves then.

DULCIE
I just need time is all!

(BESS dabs DULCIE's face with her apron, drying the tears)

BESS
...all this bawling...ruins a perfectly lovely face, you ask me.

DULCIE
You think I'm pretty?

BESS
Like a lady's portrait, you are.

DULCIE
My da said I was only good for my tits and my slit.

(Beat. BESS goes back to cleaning her face)

DULCIE
He said men paid extra for nice tits.

(Beat)

DULCIE
I was a whore.

BESS
I puzzled it out, dear.

(BESS stands back)

BESS
And you're cleaned up. Now watch me.

(She goes back to icing the pastry. DULCIE sits there. BESS waves her over)

BESS
Come. Come come come.

(DULCIE walks over)

BESS
The trick with gilding is you want to wait til the very end. The heat off the bread helps soak it in. You see?

(DULCIE nods)

BESS
Now, I put the rose water in to cut some of the oiliness. You want it to spread smooth and even, not to separate. Here. Mix.

(She hands DULCIE the bowl with the icing, then the rose water)

BESS
Make sure to mix them thoroughly.

(DULCIE does so with vigor. BESS inspects the Marchpane, then checks DULCIE's mixing)

BESS
Very good.

DULCIE
Yeah?

BESS
Smooth, even strokes. That's the key.

DULCIE
...smooth even strokes...smooth even strokes....

BESS
So do you like Nottingham?

DULCIE
I do. Never seen a place like this before. That is, I seen 'em from far away, but to be inside...

BESS
I've lived here my whole life, you know.

DULCIE
No!

BESS
God's truth. Born into the life, as it were. My

mother was the cook here before me.

DULCIE
You're a lucky one then. Never havin' to sleep in the street. Or fight off rats, or…

BESS
Oh, I've battled my share of rats.

DULCIE
Not like me. City rats big as your arm, all scabby and black. They ain't afraid of nothin'. You can scream at 'em, hit 'em…doesn't make a difference. Been bit myself, more than a few times.

BESS
That's awful.

DULCIE
That's life outside these walls, ma'am.

BESS
Now that the war is over, perhaps that will change.

DULCIE
I'll pray for the day.

BESS
We have peace now, for the first time in my life and yours. Things will change.

DULCIE
There's too much needs to be done, and not enough left alive to do it.

BESS
For now.

DULCIE
"For now," she says. Too many dead to even fill the king's kitchen proper.

BESS
Edward and his retinue weren't hardly here, so who's to care? Soon enough, the larder will be full again. A king at peace is a king at home.

DULCIE
They said the plague was done ten years ago. Then they say it's up again in the South. We bled the living, burned the dead, and still it's comin'.

BESS
That's washer-woman talk and nothing more.

DULCIE
You say that 'cause you were in here. I was out there when the Plague came. People loaded into pits 'cause there was too many to bury proper.

BESS
We suffered in these walls too.

(She takes the icing from DULCIE & tastes it)

DULCIE
Well?

BESS
It will have to do.

(BESS throws a few more items into the mix. DULCIE opens the door, listening to the music outside with pleasure)

DULCIE
Never been to a real party before.

(BESS shuts the door)

BESS
And you're not at this one either. We're here to

serve, not to participate.

DULCIE
I like the music.

BESS
It's lovely, but it's not our concern.

DULCIE
Are all those people the King's relations?

(BESS laughs a little at that)

BESS
No, dear. They're nobles who served the King during the war.

DULCIE
Oh.

BESS
They're celebrating the signing of the treaty.

DULCIE
The one that says the King is only King of England? Not King of France?

BESS
That's the one.

DULCIE
Seems queer, soldiers celebratin' peace.

BESS
They're celebrating because England is a much larger place now that the treaty is signed.

(Beat. DULCIE thinks on that)

DULCIE
So instead of being King of France, King Edward

just took part of France and called it England?

(BESS shrugs)

DULCIE
Still seems queer.

(MIRIAM enters, adjusting her skirts)

BESS
Lord be praised. I thought you'd forgotten you worked here.

MIRIAM
I'm sorry.

BESS
Be sorry while you gild the Marchpane.

(MIRIAM takes the bowl from DULCIE and starts to help ice the Marchpane. DULCIE sniffs the air)

MIRIAM
What?

DULCIE
Nothing.

BESS
Is something burning?

DULCIE
No. Not that.

(DULCIE looks at MIRIAM)

DULCIE
You been bedded.

(MIRIAM freezes, the immediately goes back to work. BESS stares at her)

MIRIAM
Nonsense.

DULCIE
You have. I know the smell.

BESS
Well, well, well...

MIRIAM
We have to get this served before Pascal has our hides.

BESS
I'm more curious about your hide.

DULCIE
Ha!

MIRIAM
Please...

BESS
It was that stablehand, wasn't it? The tall one.

MIRIAM
It was no one. Because I did nothing.

(DULCIE pulls some straw from MIRIAM's hair)

DULCIE
Then ya done nothing in the stables.

(MIRIAM grabs it as the other women laugh at her)

MIRIAM
We have work to do.

BESS
I must say, you've got me flummoxed.

MIRIAM
I'm not admitting to anything.

DULCIE
Don't have to. The proof is in the pudding.

(MIRIAM *turns, shocked at* DULCIE's *turn of phrase.* BESS *laughs*)

BESS
You've got a wicked tongue, you do.

DULCIE
You don't know the half.

MIRIAM
We have to get this bloody Marchpane ready!

(*They are silenced. They work quietly for a bit*)

DULCIE
No shame in it.

MIRIAM
Hush.

DULCIE
I done it more times than I can count. In worse places than a stable, and that's God's truth.

MIRIAM
Your council is not requested.

DULCIE
Done it on a pile of kindling once. Got splinters high and low.

BESS
Lord, you've got me missing my William.

DULCIE
Done it with a man still in his armor. Took some

effort, that did.

MIRIAM
What?

(DULCIE nods)

DULCIE
Chaffed me something awful. But he paid his way.

BESS
My William was a rough man. I loved him for that.

MIRIAM
Ladies, the Marchpane…

BESS
A good man, though. Never hurt me. Much.

(DULCIE & BESS laugh at that. Even MIRIAM smirks a little)

MIRIAM
A generation is only redeemed by the grace of the righteous women in it.

BESS
That's from your Jew book, isn't it?

MIRIAM
One of them.

DULCIE
You're a Jew?

MIRIAM
I am.

(BEAT. DULCIE just stares at MIRIAM)

MIRIAM
What?

DULCIE
Never seen a Jew before.

MIRIAM
Contrary to the folk stories, we do not have horns or cloven feet.

DULCIE
I was wonderin'.

MIRIAM
I'm just like you.

DULCIE
Can't be.

MIRIAM
Why not?

DULCIE
Because you're a Jew.

MIRIAM
(looking to BESS) Bess. Help.

(BESS moves DULCIE away)

BESS
Let's clear away the bowls, shall we?

DULCIE
So Jews can roll with regular folk?

BESS
They can. And from the looks of things, have.

DULCIE
Ha!

MIRIAM
How is this helping?

DULCIE
Was he no good at it, then?

MIRIAM
He was fine and...We are not discussing this!

DULCIE
So did you ride him or did he ride you?

MIRIAM
I beg your pardon?!

DULCIE
Come marchin' in here covered in straw, and I'm not supposed to ask?

BESS
Well, judging by the straw in her hair...

DULCIE
She was on bottom.

BESS
Precisely.

MIRIAM
I long for the moment when we're speaking of something else. Anything else.

DULCIE
You seemed so prim and proper, you did.

BESS
What's the boy's name...? Richard? Roland?

MIRIAM
...Robert...

(All laugh at that)

DULCIE
Ooooo! I know the one you mean! Walks around like he needs a cart to carry it.

BESS
Always had his eye on you. I never thought you'd give him a chance. Voila!

(She steps away from the Marchpane. They all examine it)

BESS
What do you think?

MIRIAM
I think if the King doesn't like it, I'm going to wish I stayed in the stable.

DULCIE
He wouldn't do nothing to us, would he?

BESS
I'd be more worried about Pascal.

DULCIE
The King's been good to me.

MIRIAM
How many times have you made Marchpane?

BESS
Hard to recall.

MIRIAM
I'm certain they'll like it.

DULCIE
Took me into the castle, made me a cook...

BESS
Christ Almighty couldn't make you a cook, girl.

DULCIE
I'm doin' my damned best!

(The door opens, and PASCAL enters. He is dressed as a high-ranking servant and moves with purpose. Though he was born in France, his accent is very slight, if present at all)

PASCAL
Well. How stands the dessert?

BESS
It passes muster.

PASCAL
Passes muster? I hope it does more than that. There are a dozen lords awaiting its presentation. And the King is in a mood this night.

DULCIE
In a mood?

(PASCAL closes on her)

PASCAL
You're the new girl, yes?

DULCIE
Dulcie Cullen, m'lord. Just got here today and...

PASCAL
I am no lord. I am King Edward's steward, and as such, you answer to me. Am I understood?

DULCIE
Yes.

(PASCAL looks at MIRIAM)

PASCAL
Your appearance is more disheveled than I'd like, Miriam.

MIRIAM
I beg your pardon, M'sieu Pascal. I was...needed in the stable.

PASCAL
Indeed? I had no idea our horses had such discriminating tastes.

MIRIAM
I wasn't...that is to say...

BESS
I sent here there, M'sieu Pascal. We needed some...hay...to stoke the fires.

(PASCAL snorts)

PASCAL
Madame, I spent my early years on a farm. As such, I know bullshit when I smell it.

(DULCIE tries not to laugh at the rude remark. PASCAL smiles a bit)

BESS
You're a right terror, you are.

PASCAL
So I've been told. Now...

(A knock on the kitchen door. PASCAL sees who it is, then turns back to the ladies)

PASCAL
Get the Marchpane prepared for serving. I'll be back in a moment.

BESS
Oui, m'sieu.

MIRIAM
Oui, m'sieu.

(He walks out)

DULCIE
Oh, I like him.

BESS
Everyone likes him. He's very charming.

DULCIE
I like all that French talk.

MIRIAM
Well, Dulcie, he is French.

DULCIE
No!

MIRIAM
Yes.

DULCIE
He don't smell it.

BESS
Aren't you quite the bloodhound?

MIRIAM
He's been in the king's service for…Bess, how long has it been?

BESS
Since before the king, in fact. Served his majesty's mother.

(BESS leads them back to the table, where they

start preparing the food for serving)

DULCIE
He's all business, too. Like that.

BESS
Eyes forward, girl.

DULCIE
…walks in like he owns us all…

(BESS smacks her on the head with a spoon)

DULCIE
Ah! Christ!

BESS
If you knock over this Marchpane, you'll meet the good Lord Christ soon enough.

DULCIE
I weren't knockin' nothin' over!

MIRIAM
She's saying you need to pay attention to your work.

BESS
Stop sniffing after Henri and get the silver.

DULCIE
(getting the silver) Who's Henri?

BESS
The French gentleman you're so taken with.

DULCIE
Pascal?

MIRIAM
Henri Pascal.

DULCIE
Oooooooh! Now, that does sound French.

(PASCAL returns, agitated)

PASCAL
How close are we?

BESS
Give me another minute. Maybe two for the flowers.

(BESS begins to decorate the setting)

PASCAL
I'll give you one. Garnish faster.

(BESS moves quicker)

MIRIAM
How is it?

PASCAL
Tense. King Edward just called the Duke of Burgundy a coward.

DULCIE
To his face?

PASCAL
To his face, and the faces of all those at the table.

BESS
Lord, he is in a mood.

PASCAL
Are you garnishing?

BESS
You want this to go faster? Get me some proper help.

PASCAL
If you are feeling short-staffed, I'd recommend you take it up with the plague.

MIRIAM
(to DULCIE) You wouldn't know it, but we had twelve women working here not so long ago.

(BESS crosses herself)

BESS
Lord, bless us and keep us well.

(PASCAL puts trays in the hands of MIRIAM & DULCIE)

PASCAL
Less chatter, if you please.

(They talk as they work)

MIRIAM
Cleaned out many of us. Bess and I were the only ones who never caught it.

PASCAL
Yes, we're all blessed with our health. Now please! Expediency!

DULCIE
I had it.

(All freeze. They see that DULCIE is touching the garnish)

BESS
The plague?

DULCIE
Aye. I can show you the pock-marks where they stuck me.

(She begins to undo her shirt)

PASCAL
No! Please! Quite unnecessary!

(BESS has moved her away from the cake, then turns on PASCAL)

BESS
You brought a sick woman into my kitchen?!

DULCIE
What?

PASCAL
I didn't hire her! She was sent here by the King!

MIRIAM
What?

DULCIE
I ain't sick no more.

PASCAL
She's some unfortunate the King took pity on...

BESS
You never told me that.

DULCIE
I ain't sick! I was sick, but not no more.

(They stare at her. Uncertain what to do, she starts to undo her shirt again)

BESS
Stop that!

DULCIE
I'm tryin' to show you. I ain't had the plague for...must be almost eleven years now.

BESS
Oh thank God.

DULCIE
Aye, thank God you should. You can't imagine it.

MIRIAM
What was it like?

DULCIE
Like walkin' around, but bein' dead. My joints all locked up…couldn't see or hear through the fever….

MIRIAM
Oh my.

DULCIE
And they bled me, too. When I got the boils. Cut right into me, and the blood that come out was black!

BESS
No!

DULCIE
Oh yes. Black, and stinkin' of filth. I see it streamin' out and I think to myself "Well, Dulcie Girl, let's hope Jesus gots a warm heart for sick girls…"

PASCAL
Ladies, while this recollection is not without its charm, there are guests who need attending to! Bess, you and the new girl bring the Marchpane to the servers.

BESS
Oui, m'sieu.

DULCIE
Oui. Yes. Oui.

PASCAL
I'd like to discuss the state of the stables with Miriam.

(Beat. They look at MIRIAM with pity, then cart up the Marchpane. PASCAL goes to the door. Beat. PASCAL laughs a bit. MIRIAM smiles)

PASCAL
They're gone.

MIRIAM
Good.

PASCAL
I thought that was rather convincing.

MIRIAM
Indeed. There was a moment where I truly feared the back of your hand.

PASCAL
Have I ever raised a hand to you?

MIRIAM
Yes. But only when I brought it on myself.

(They embrace)

MIRIAM
How much time do we have?

PASCAL
It will take at least five minutes to see them all served.

MIRIAM
Good. And your contact? Was he among the

Baron's retinue?

PASCAL
Yes. An odious, unpleasant fellow, but true to his word.

MIRIAM
Then you have it?

PASCAL
I do.

(He scans the room quickly, then pulls a ring out of his pocket)

MIRIAM
This is it, then.

PASCAL
Yes.

MIRIAM
(inspecting it) Show me.

(He unhooks a small lock, and the ring opens)

PASCAL
Careful now. That's monkshood leaves, ground to a powder.

MIRIAM
Deadly then?

PASCAL
Extremely. But the effects are not immediate.

MIRIAM
What? But we discussed...

PASCAL
No, this is a good thing. If the King were to feel the effects at once, he might call out for help.

But monkshood...he'll likely fall asleep before he feels a thing.

(He closes the ring, but keeps it in his hand)

PASCAL
Miriam. You have to let me do this.

MIRIAM
No.

PASCAL
It will be easy enough for me. Trying to find a way to get you into the King's chambers...

MIRIAM
I am doing this, Henri. I have to do this.

PASCAL
I am an old man. I can...

MIRIAM
Do not try to take this from me.

(Beat. PASCAL sees her deadly seriousness)

PASCAL
So be it. The King takes a glass of wine before he sleeps. Sometimes more. That will be the key.

MIRIAM
I know.

PASCAL
When I feel he's ready to turn in, I shall fetch you.

MIRIAM
I know all this, Henri.

PASCAL
And you shall hear me tell it to you again, one

more time. There can be no mistake.

(She concedes)

PASCAL
Do you remember how to get to the hidden tunnel?

MIRIAM
Behind the third tapestry in the foyer.

PASCAL
It will lead you directly to his room. Take a candle, it will be dark.

MIRIAM
Of course.

PASCAL
I will delay the King from his chambers as best I can. You must sneak in quickly, and empty the entire contents of this ring into his bottle. All of it. Do you understand?

MIRIAM
I do. Are you certain monkshood will suffice?

PASCAL
Oh yes. So long as he remains undisturbed, it will appear that his heart seized in the night. Once you've poisoned the drink, go quickly through the tunnel again and meet me at my chambers.

MIRIAM
Wouldn't it draw less suspicion if I simply returned to my chambers?

PASCAL
Do it for me. So that I know you're safe.

(Beat)

MIRIAM
All right.

PASCAL
If all goes well, then the King will never even know you were there.

MIRIAM
And if all does not go well?

PASCAL
Spare an old man and say no more.

(He pats her head affectionately, then finds a piece of straw. He looks at her, awaiting an explanation)

MIRIAM
It may be my last day on earth.

PASCAL
I don't like that sort of talk.

MIRIAM
Robert has been chasing me around since I was old enough to notice.

(She can sense his anger rising)

MIRIAM
Don't.

PASCAL
I'll thrash him into oblivion.

MIRIAM
This was my choice.

PASCAL
You're a girl! A child! And he took advantage of that!

MIRIAM
Henri. Stop.

(She takes his hand. His anger fades)

MIRIAM
I'm no girl. I've been a woman for years now.

PASCAL
Of course. I simply…

MIRIAM
I wanted this to happen. It was my choice, and I do not regret it.

PASCAL
Virtue is a thing not to be tossed aside lightly.

MIRIAM
It wasn't. I promise you.

PASCAL
Your life does not end here. Not tonight, not in this place.

MIRIAM
It could.

PASCAL
It won't.

MIRIAM
Are you a prophet now? Has God granted you a vision from above?

PASCAL
He has granted me age and wisdom. We've planned this well. We'll both survive the night.

MIRIAM
We may. He will not.

PASCAL
On that, we are agreed.

(He sits, weary. She brings him some water)

MIRIAM
This weighs heavy on you.

PASCAL
It does.

MIRIAM
He's a monster.

PASCAL
He was young once. Just like you. I knew him then. And served him well.

MIRIAM
Serpents begin as children too. It doesn't make them any less deadly.

PASCAL
You worry me, Miriam.

MIRIAM
Why?

PASCAL
Because this does weigh heavily on me, but does not seem to weigh upon you at all.

MIRIAM
I will see justice done. My soul is clean.

(He laughs a sad laugh)

PASCAL
This is not justice. In a world where beasts devour their young and a pinch of powder can fell a king…no, justice is a mortal invention. What you

feel…what you will do this night…is something more primal.

MIRIAM
Vengeance.

(He nods)

PASCAL
Vengeance.

(MIRIAM sits with him, rests her head on shoulder)

MIRIAM
I know you cared for him. Perhaps you still do. But this has to be done, Henri. England cannot endure another war. This peace will not last, not so long as Edward lives.

PASCAL
I know it. God help me, I do. I just cannot comprehend that it has come to this.

MIRIAM
It began before I was even born, on a road turned red by the blood of the English…

PASCAL
And the French.

MIRIAM
Yes. And the French.

(He lets that sink in, regaining some of his drive)

PASCAL
You were right to insist on doing this yourself. An assassin must be unflinching in her determination.

MIRIAM
You know I do not like that word.

PASCAL
And sheep don't like the word mutton.

MIRIAM
Ever the wit.

(He rises, crosses to the door)

PASCAL
This is a good night for it. The castle will be full of many of Edward's friends. Friends who would cut out his heart for a chance at power.

MIRIAM
Who would suspect one of his cooks?

PASCAL
Precisely. He will not be the first Plantagenet to meet their end in this castle. There's a certain poetry to that, don't you think?

MIRIAM
I leave poetry to the Irish.

(She crosses to PASCAL & holds out her hand)

PASCAL
Are you trying to show me something very small?

MIRIAM
The ring, m'sieu.

PASCAL
Ah. Of course.

(He reaches into his pocket, hands the ring to her)

MIRIAM
I can't decide if you're absent minded or overly-protective.

PASCAL
I think you know.

(She kisses his cheek)

MIRIAM
You would have been a fine father, Henri.

PASCAL
Oh, I suppose we'll never know.

(She embraces him tightly. He holds her, knowing it may be the last time)

MIRIAM
I know.

(The door swings open, and they quickly release each other. DULCIE walks in, soaking wet)

DULCIE
Christ! Now that's a rain!

PASCAL
Oh come now! This is no way for a king's cook to appear!

DULCIE
Not my fault! The rain's fault!

MIRIAM
Are the windows open?!

DULCIE
No, no. Nothin' like that. The king went outside.

PASCAL
He what?

DULCIE
Hand to god. Middle of dessert, he got all sullen-like. Just stood up, without saying a word, and walked right out into the downpour.

PASCAL
Mon dieu me protègent...

(PASCAL bolts out the door, running into BESS. She is wet, but much less so than DULCIE)

BESS
Oh! Beg pardon, M'sieu...

PASCAL
One side, woman.

(PASCAL is gone. BESS sees DULCIE)

BESS
Good lord, girl. Stand by the fire!

(DULCIE does so)

BESS
It's not so hard a thing to throw on a cloak before you stomp into the tempest!

DULCIE
It was all the excitement!

(She speaks to MIRIAM)

DULCIE
You shoulda seen it! All the guards runnin' about, them noble-types soaked to the bone. No one could get him to come inside. The King, I mean. Him just standin' there, shoutin' at the sky.

MIRIAM
He...what?

BESS
It's the truth, dear. His majesty just stood there, howling against the rain and thunder. It was quite a sight to behold.

MIRIAM
Why on earth would he do that?

BESS
Haven't a clue. Pascal said there was something off about him all night. He was just sittin' there, like the girl said. Next thing we know, he knocks over the Marchpane and...

(Beat)

BESS
Oh god! My Marchpane!

(BESS starts to go, MIRIAM stops her)

MIRIAM
I'll tend to it. Go dry yourself.

(MIRIAM goes off. BESS joins DULCIE by the fire)

DULCIE
I tell ya, miss. I like workin' here. So exciting.

BESS
It's not always like this. Fact, it's almost never like this.

DULCIE
Shame, that. A girl can get used to it.

BESS
I'd think your past employment was excitement enough.

DULCIE
Oh, no. Got awful boring.

(They warm themselves by the fire)

DULCIE
Ooo, that warms the nethers, don't it?

BESS
I don't know if this fire is up to the task of warming my old bones. What I'd give for a proper bath.

DULCIE
That sounds lovely.

(BESS crosses away, begins to clean dishes)

DULCIE
I meant to ask ya…is that little bit your girl?

BESS
Miriam?

(DULCIE nods)

BESS
Might as well be. Her mother passed…oh, must be almost thirteen years now. I raised her as much as anyone. In fact, I was there the day she was born.

DULCIE
Yeah?

BESS
Two months early. Oh, we were all of us on our knees praying. A babe born early, during the plague…they didn't last long. But Miriam's got fire in her.

DULCIE
Huh. She looks like she'd break in a strong wind.

BESS
Her father was that way. No bigger around than a sapling. The King couldn't remember his name for the longest time. Kept calling him Little Jew.

DULCIE
Christ! This fire'll never do! I'm still a drippin' mess!

(MIRIAM enters)

BESS
My...my Marchpane?

(MIRIAM shakes her head "No.")

BESS
Well. Perfect. I spend half the night assembling the finest dessert a King could ask for, and he goes mad and ruins it. Perfect.

(DULCIE puts her arms around her)

DULCIE
It's all right. There's no way you could've known.

(Beat)

BESS
Was I not damp enough before?

(DULCIE steps back)

DULCIE
Right. Sorry. I...why don't I go put on my dry clothes? *(exits)*

BESS
Sweet girl, that one. But dim as a candle without a wick.

MIRIAM
She seems all right.

BESS
You say that because you were off romping in the hay while I was here, keeping her from burning down my kitchen.

MIRIAM
I'm sure it wasn't that bad.

BESS
Miriam, have you ever known me to exaggerate?

(MIRIAM chuckles at that)

MIRIAM
Sometimes, I'm not sure you do anything but.

(BESS hands her a large pot)

BESS
Just for that, the pots are yours.

MIRIAM
Bess...

BESS
Oh, I'm certain your young, strong fingers will be able to reach the spots these old talons can't.

MIRIAM
You're fortunate I think of you fondly.

BESS
Ha! Little twig of a thing like you making threats. There's the laugh I've needed.

MIRIAM
You think me harmless?

BESS
A kitten may have claws, but they can't sink very deep.

MIRIAM
So I'm a kitten, am I?

BESS
Do a good job on the pots and I'll set out a saucer of milk.

(They clean for a bit, silently enjoying each other's company)

BESS
Did you see the King?

MIRIAM
I saw Pascal leading him to his bedchamber.

BESS
Off to draw him a steaming hot bath, I'd wager.

MIRIAM
Why would he just stand there in the storm?

BESS
Not for us to ask.

MIRIAM
I'm not asking him, Bess. I'm not at his door, demanding an audience. I'm asking you.

BESS
I'm not one to engage in idle speculation.

MIRIAM
Ha!

BESS
Well…not about his majesty, at least.

MIRIAM
Oh? And what places him above your reproachful eye?

BESS
What sort of question is that? He's our King.

MIRIAM
He's a man. He fights, he drinks, he shits, just like any other.

(BESS shakes her head, thinking)

BESS
The King is the land, the land is the King.

MIRIAM
What?

BESS
Your father was the one who told me that. The two are eternally intertwined.

MIRIAM
That's daft.

BESS
I just wonder...that storm tonight. It's brutal... most brutal I've seen in years. And I think...is the land raging as the King rages?

MIRIAM
It's just a storm.

BESS
Not so sure about that.

MIRIAM
Besides, he has no reason to rage. He has declared peace.

BESS
A hard thing to imagine. I can't remember a time when the war wasn't at least threatening.

MIRIAM
You think it will start again?

BESS
No. Both sides have something. France has their own king, and England has new lands.

MIRIAM
After all this time, you'd think victory would be something more...

BESS
Monumental?

MIRIAM
Yes.

(BESS shakes her head)

BESS
When it goes on as long as this, no one can truly recall why it was started in the first place. Still, Edward led us well.

(MIRIAM slams down the pot she was cleaning, trying to control her rising anger)

MIRIAM
He led Englishmen to their death, over and over, soldiers and peasants both! I wonder if they would share your sentiment.

BESS
It was his duty as king. And I should remind you that it's his name inked onto the treaty. I think the great losses have weighed on him long enough.

(Beat. MIRIAM stares at BESS)

MIRIAM
You're concerned over him?

BESS
Of course I am. He's my liege. And our livelihood.

(MIRIAM just snorts at that)

BESS
I know he's the only King you have ever known, Miri. But I remember when the Regent Mortimer ruled in his stead. Those were darker days than this.

MIRIAM
Indeed?

BESS
Oh yes. The regent was a right and bloody bastard. Cruel to all around him. He cared nothing for this kingdom, only his own power. I was just a girl when Edward crept back into this castle and claimed his rightful throne. And I cheered when he did.

MIRIAM
Knowing that you'd traded a petty tyrant for a warmonger?

BESS
Edward loves his land, and his people. He is our king by divine right.

MIRIAM
No. No! Do not speak to me of divine right! Do not tell me that God has looked at the rotting corpses in the field and blessed the butcher's handiwork. God washed his hands of kings and

regents long ago.

BESS
That's a dangerous way to think.

MIRIAM
Or is it difficult to watch someone think at all, after a lifetime of servile obedience?

(BESS slaps MIRIAM)

BESS
Who am I?

MIRIAM
What?

BESS
Who am I? To you? Am I some addle-minded sheep who needs your shepherding? Or am I the woman who raised you, who taught you your trade?

MIRIAM
You are not my mother.

BESS
For the better part of your life, I was all the mother you'd ever known. Talk to me like that again and I'll black your eye for you.

(MIRIAM rises, fuming)

BESS
Now hold on. I did that 'cause I love you.

MIRIAM
You can love me all you like, but you know nothing of me. You know nothing of how my people have suffered.

BESS
Nor do you.

(MIRIAM stops, too shocked to answer)

BESS
Your father came to this court seeking sanctuary for himself and your mother. I know the way Jews have been run out, spit on, and killed. But that has never happened to you here, nor will it. And if your father were still here, you'd be thanking him for it.

MIRIAM
My father is not here. And his safe world here didn't protect him in the end.

BESS
I know that. And there's not a day goes by that I don't miss him. He was a sweet man, and a gentle spirit. There was a time when you were much the same.

(MIRIAM goes back to cleaning)

BESS
There was also a time when there were no secrets between us, Miri.

MIRIAM
I wasn't aware that time had passed.

BESS
I've seen you.

(MIRIAM stops, stares at BESS)

BESS
You walk through these halls like a shadow. There's a darkness deep inside you that scares me to look

at. I worry that it's taken over the knock-kneed girl who sang from the tower tops.

MIRIAM
I'm not a girl anymore. I can bring in Robert to attest to that, if you'd like.

(Beat. BESS can't help but laugh at that. MIRIAM smiles)

BESS
You've your father's wicked tongue.

MIRIAM
I know. I only pray I don't inherit his beard as well.

(BESS rubs MIRIAM's chin)

BESS
Oh, I think you're well on your way.

(MIRIAM bats her hand away. They smile, some of the tension passing)

MIRIAM
Did he love the King? My father?

BESS
Oh yes. Very much.

MIRIAM
Why?

BESS
Because he was king.

MIRIAM
No. My father was not one to give loyalty lightly.

BESS
Best not to ask why. Just go about your work.

MIRIAM
In all the years I've known you, I've never seen you decline a story.

BESS
It's not much of a story to tell, really. Probably best to...

MIRIAM
Bess. Please.

(Beat)

BESS
I have a hard time keeping my tongue from wagging, I know. I'm a woman of few secrets. Let me keep this one.

MIRIAM
If it concerns my father, I want to know. I deserve to know.

(BESS pauses, about to tell a story she never wanted to tell)

BESS
You were but a babe, so I doubt you remember this. When your mother grew ill...she was the first in the castle to do so. And many of the servants, not me mind you, they...God help me, they wanted her burned.

MIRIAM
What?

BESS
It's awful, I know. But they were panicked, and panic spreads faster than any pox. She had the boils on her neck, and there was no hiding them. One night...

(BESS sits, finding it difficult to tell)

BESS
One night, while the King was on the field...do you remember Peter, the blacksmith?

(MIRIAM shakes her head no)

BESS
No reason you should, I suppose. Well, one night he roused the other smiths and...I was asleep at the time. My William wakes me up. There's an awful racket coming from down the hall. We open the door to see Peter and his boys dragging your ma out of her room. Your father is fighting as best he can, but he couldn't hold against them. Peter and them...they take your mother to the smithy outside. They've got the fires roaring and...we all know what they mean to do. I'm throwin' rocks by now, but it's doing no good. The great bastard keeps yelling that he's doin' this for all of us, trying to keep us safe. Your father presses you into my arms, and charges the man. Well, he gets maybe two steps, and suddenly Peter stops cold. He makes this queer, choking noise, and drops your mother. Well, he's makin' that noise 'cause he has an arrow sticking through his throat. The King had come home early, seen what was going on, and he took care of it, just as a king should. He helped your ma up, lead her right back to her husband. Told all of us to go back to our chambers, and if there's any more talk of burning the sick, well...he had a whole quiver full of arrows should it come to that.

(MIRIAM sits in silence for a long time, her emotions erratic)

MIRIAM
Why did you tell me this?

BESS
You asked.

MIRIAM
Then...why didn't you tell me before tonight?

(BESS takes her hand)

BESS
Because I love you like you're one of my own. And if I could've taken that story with me to the grave, I would have. There's some things that are best left buried.

(MIRIAM knocks away the cup in front of her, unable to control her rage)

MIRIAM
I know what this is.

BESS
Miriam!

MIRIAM
You seek to stop me, to make me...no! This changes nothing! Do you hear me?

BESS
Calm down, girl!

MIRIAM
I have waited too long, done things that...god...

(She can take no more, doubles over and weeps. BESS cradles her)

BESS
Oh god forgive me, I should never have told you.

MIRIAM
...let me go...

BESS
I been carrying that tale with me too long. I just didn't want to add another moment of pain to your life.

MIRIAM
Bess...there is something inside me...in my mind...

BESS
Shhh. Shhh. Just breathe, lamb.

MIRIAM
I don't know who I am anymore.

BESS
That's just your grief talking.

MIRIAM
It's not. God help me, it's not. *(She grabs BESS' face)* I've lost the girl I once was. And I do not know if I want her found.

BESS
Never lost.

MIRIAM
You cannot take my hate from me, Bess. You cannot.

BESS
Miri, listen to yourself.

MIRIAM
It is all I have!

BESS
You have me. You have Pascal.

MIRIAM
You don't know what it's like, to give yourself to hatred. Utterly and completely. It is my clarity, my strength.

BESS
You just need to sit.

(In a sudden motion, MIRIAM takes a kitchen knife and stabs it hard into the table. BESS sits there stunned)

MIRIAM
Had my father been a stronger man, he would've done that to the blacksmith's heart.

BESS
I think that night he would have. And I don't know if he ever would have forgiven himself.

MIRIAM
When murder is just, forgiveness isn't needed.

BESS
You don't believe that.

MIRIAM
I know it. In my skin, my muscles, my bones... I know it more than I've ever known anything else.

BESS
Miri...

MIRIAM
For an innocent life lost, a guilty life is forfeit, be it peasant or king.

(Beat. BESS finally understands what MIRIAM intends)

BESS
No.

MIRIAM
Do not stop me, Bess.

BESS
What you're thinking...you'll die.

MIRIAM
His corpse will go cold before mine.

BESS
Oh my god. Why would you...?

MIRIAM
Why?! Do you need to ask me that? You of all people know why this must be done, and why I must be the one to do it.

BESS
Your father would never have wanted this.

MIRIAM
Is that what you think?! Because I suspect that while he laid there, bleeding to death, the skin flayed from his body...I suspect this is exactly what he wanted.

BESS
Then you never knew him.

MIRIAM
And you did? You had some insight into my father that I never possessed?

BESS
I wouldn't have thought so before this night.

MIRIAM
So this is it, then. Do you stop me, or do you let

me go?

(BESS has no answer, unsure)

MIRIAM
If you report me to the King, then I die. If you do nothing, then he dies.

BESS
No. I don't accept that.

MIRIAM
You must.

BESS
You cannot heap death at my feat, death not of my making, and call it mine. Are you truly so far gone?

MIRIAM
Farther than you know.

(BESS stands in front of the door)

BESS
What if I were to do nothing but stand here? Would you kill me to get through?

(Beat)

MIRIAM
I think not. But I'd rather not put it to the test.

(Suddenly, the door swings open and DULCIE walks in, her clothes dry)

DULCIE
Oh. Sorry. Did I miss the cleaning?

MIRIAM
Leave us.

DULCIE
You got no say ordering me around. You're just a cook, same as me.

BESS
Yes, Miriam. You're just a cook. Nothing more.

MIRIAM
Dulcie. Get out.

DULCIE
What's this then? A squabble? Well, you two can squabble around me all you'd like. I know when to listen and when not to.

BESS
I think it would be better if Dulcie stayed, dear. And this is still my kitchen.

MIRIAM
Then I shall take my leave.

(BESS stands in the doorway, defiant. They glare at each other)

BESS
You're not done with your cleaning.

MIRIAM
Out of my way, old woman.

BESS
You're. Not. Done.

(They stare each other down. Finally, MIRIAM returns to her cleaning. A long silence hangs in the room. Finally, DULCIE speaks)

DULCIE
Queer night though, isn't it? Must be the storm.

MIRIAM
Yes. That must be it.

DULCIE
At least the King seems to be back in his right mind. Seen Pascal talking to him.

MIRIAM
What?

BESS
Leave it be.

DULCIE
Yeah, the two goin' on like old friends. I was glad to see it.

MIRIAM
What were they saying?

DULCIE
(shrugs) Not my place to listen, so I didn't.

(BESS hands MIRIAM more dishes)

DULCIE
All I knows is the King seemed glad for it. Relieved. That's the word. Relieved.

(MIRIAM starts to go. BESS stops her)

BESS
The King's men have no need of you, nor do his guards. Stay and finish cleaning.

MIRIAM
I am done here.

BESS
You're done if you leave. Get back to the basin and clean. Dulcie, watch her.

(MIRIAM *goes back, her panic mounting.* DULCIE, *noting the tension, speaks in hushed tones to* MIRIAM. *As they speak,* BESS *takes an armload of items back to the cellar*)

DULCIE
What's happened?

MIRIAM
Nothing.

DULCIE
You two was thick as thieves when I left. Now there's razors between you.

MIRIAM
We fought. It's not uncommon.

DULCIE
I'd say it is.

MIRIAM
Quiet. I need to think.

DULCIE
Old Bess...she's a fighter. I still got a lump from where she brained me with a spoon. But you...

MIRIAM
Quiet!

DULCIE
You're just a little slip of a girl.

MIRIAM
You have no concept of what I am.

DULCIE
Ha! I seen things on the streets that you'd never believe. I seen a man choke his newborn babe for cryin' too loud. Seen a starving woman beat a dog

to death, just to have it for a meal. I know where that sort of desperation lives…

(She taps her head)

DULCIE
…in here. And I know that it don't live in you.

(MIRIAM stares at DULCIE, unsure as to how much the other woman knows DULCIE laughs a little)

DULCIE
Kinda poetical, yeah? Well, I'll leave poetry to the Irish.

(Beat. MIRIAM makes sure BESS is still off reshelving supplies)

MIRIAM
What do you want from me?

DULCIE
How's that?

MIRIAM
I know you know. What will it take to let me go out that door?

DULCIE
Probably just pullin' the handle. I don't think…

(MIRIAM grabs DULCIE roughly)

DULCIE
Hey!

MIRIAM
Don't fence with me. I am set on my purpose.

DULCIE
Get off of me!

(MIRIAM grabs the knife from the table and holds it to DULCIE's throat)

DULCIE
Christ!

MIRIAM
Quiet, damn you. Or I'll slit you ear to ear.

DULCIE
I ain't done nothin'. You got no cause to kill me.

MIRIAM
What does the King know?

DULCIE
How should I know?

MIRIAM
What did you tell him?

DULCIE
What?!

(MIRIAM presses the blade in a bit)

MIRIAM
What did you tell him?

(DULCIE begins to weep quietly)

DULCIE
I told him that I love him. That's all.

MIRIAM
What?

DULCIE
When he lay with me…that's all I said. And I could hardly say even that.

(MIRIAM releases her, but still keeps the knife

pointed at her)

MIRIAM
When was this?

DULCIE
A few days back. When he found me.

(DULCIE reads MIRIAM's puzzled expression)

DULCIE
What d'ya think I'm here for? My cooking? I put salt into jam for Christ's sake.

MIRIAM
You're his whore?

DULCIE
Not no more. Well, not a whore no more. He found me in the streets, saw the life I was living and took me away from it. If he wants a roll now and then... What? He never rolled with you?

MIRIAM
No!

DULCIE
Hardly a surprise there, pullin' knives like that. Still, the way I hear tell, it's only a matter of time. He's worked his way through half the castle already, so they say.

(BESS returns. She sees MIRIAM with the knife)

BESS
Oh God! What have you done?

MIRIAM
Nothing.

(BESS inspects DULCIE)

BESS
Did she hurt you?

DULCIE
Close bloody enough. You keep that rabid bitch away from me.

MIRIAM
You said yourself I was without desperation.

DULCIE
Then I take it back!

(BESS notices the small nick on DULCIE's neck)

BESS
You drew her blood.

MIRIAM
A drop or two at most.

DULCIE
You…what?!

(DULCIE sees the blood for herself)

DULCIE
You bloody cunt!

(She charges MIRIAM. BESS intercedes. She pushes DULCIE onto a stool)

BESS
Do not move, Dulcie Cullen, unless you want a cracked skull.

DULCIE
But she…

BESS
Not an inch.

(DULCIE is silent. BESS turns to MIRIAM)

BESS
I cannot keep you here.

(Beat)

MIRIAM
I know.

BESS
I love you dearly. You know that?

MIRIAM
I do.

BESS
But you'll bring the King's guard on us before long.

(MIRIAM nods)

BESS
I'll give you this night. Collect some things, and I'll make you some food. But you sleep in my chambers. I'll not have you sneaking off.

(MIRIAM just stares, saying nothing)

BESS
In the morning, I'll speak to Pascal about having you dismissed.

DULCIE
You think you've had it rough here? You don't know. The world's a cruel place beyond the castle walls.

MIRIAM
Perhaps it's time I discovered that myself.

(BESS goes to her, touches MIRIAM's face. Her heart is breaking)

BESS
You were a child once. Not so long ago. How did you become this?

(She takes BESS' hand)

MIRIAM
It's not for you to know.

(PASCAL enters, shaken)

BESS
M'sieu Pascal.

DULCIE
M'sieu.

BESS
I'm sorry we're behind on our cleaning, sir.

PASCAL
It is of no importance.

BESS
We had an...incident tonight.

DULCIE
That witch tried to cut my throat!

BESS
Be silent!

PASCAL
Miriam...

BESS
Let us clean up here, then I'd like to talk to you in the morning.

PASCAL
There will be no need for that.

(PASCAL looks at MIRIAM)

PASCAL
Miriam. The King requests your presence.

(Lights fade)

END OF ACT I

ACT II

(The King's bedchamber. It is opulent, with a large bed, a table with a bottle & goblets, and a large window. EDWARD stands at the wine table. He is dressed in nightclothes, but is still in every way a consummate general. He is tall and strong, with long graying hair and a beard. PASCAL and MIRIAM stand before him)

EDWARD
Tell me of this girl, Pascal.

PASCAL
This is Miriam, one of your cooks.

EDWARD
Hmm.

PASCAL
She is the daughter of Saul.

(EDWARD looks at PASCAL, momentarily unsure who Saul is. Then--)

EDWARD
Ah! The Little Jew!

PASCAL
Yes, sire.

EDWARD
He was a good man, your father. And a sharp mind. Numbers, languages…how he held it all in his tiny head I'll never know.

MIRIAM
Yes, sire.

EDWARD
Well, let's have a look at you then.

(EDWARD walks to her)

EDWARD
Look at me.

(She does so. He takes her chin, lifting her head a bit so that he's looking directly down on her)

EDWARD
Your face is pretty enough. A bit plain. Teeth.

(She does nothing, unsure what he means)

EDWARD
Show me your teeth.

(She opens her mouth)

EDWARD
You're not a horse, child. Just smile.

(She does so)

EDWARD
Good teeth. Even. Were you ever plagued?

(She looks to PASCAL)

EDWARD
Don't look at him. Answer me. Did the Black Death touch you?

MIRIAM
No. It claimed my mother. I was spared. Sire.

EDWARD
She was not alone in that. I damn near lost my castle to the deaths.

MIRIAM
Is a mother worth less than a castle?

(PASCAL shoots her a worried look. EDWARD laughs)

EDWARD
Look at what I did to my own mother. I think that should answer the question. Pascal, this girl has a sharp tongue. Has she ever given you trouble?

PASCAL
Nothing of note, sire.

EDWARD
Why do I find that difficult to believe?

PASCAL
She speaks her mind unbidden. It is not a charming quality. But she is an excellent cook and maid.

EDWARD
Your father was very much the same way, Marian. He had opinions on everything, and had trouble keeping them to himself.

MIRIAM
Miriam.

EDWARD
What's that?

PASCAL
Girl...

MIRIAM
My name is Miriam, not Marian.

(The king closes on her, towering over her)

EDWARD
If I decide you are Marian, than you are Marian. Understood?

MIRIAM
Yes, sire.

(For the first time, he notices her ring. He lifts her hand. PASCAL tenses)

EDWARD
A lovely bauble. Not something often allowed a servant.

MIRIAM
It was my mother's, sire.

EDWARD
Was it now?

(She begins to remove it)

MIRIAM
If you'd rather I not wear it...

EDWARD
Keep it. It is of no consequence.

(EDWARD stares at MIRIAM for a long time, taking her in)

EDWARD
Pascal, you may leave us.

PASCAL
As you wish, sire.

(PASCAL bows, locking eyes with MIRIAM. He then exits. EDWARD pours himself a goblet of wine)

EDWARD
How old are you, girl?

MIRIAM
Twenty.

(He drinks the wine)

EDWARD
A good year.

(He removes his robe)

EDWARD
Do I scare you?

MIRIAM
No, sire.

(Beat)

MIRIAM
Yes, sire.

EDWARD
And why is that?

MIRIAM
You are the king. I am...nothing.

EDWARD
Look up.

(She looks at him)

EDWARD
I'm not the Virgin Mary, you needn't avert your eyes.

MIRIAM
I was taught...

EDWARD
I will not speak with someone who will not look me in the eyes.

(He goes to her, puts his hands on arms and looks deep into her eyes. He is looking for something within her)

EDWARD
When you look a man in the eyes, Miriam, they have a difficult time holding onto their secrets. Those who glance downward often have daggers in their sleeves.

MIRIAM
Or perhaps they are simply beneath your station.

EDWARD
The two are not mutually exclusive.

(He pours her a glass of wine. She takes it but does not drink. He drinks as he talks)

EDWARD
You said you are nothing, am I right?

MIRIAM
You are, sire.

EDWARD
Stop!

(She freezes)

EDWARD
Stop calling me "sire". I'm in no mood for it.

(She stands there, silent)

EDWARD
So you think you are nothing. What is that like?

MIRIAM
I'm not sure I understand.

EDWARD
My entire life, I was bred to rule. I knew I was to be king before I knew how to spell my name. I'm curious what it feels like to know you are destined for nothing at all.

MIRIAM
I have nothing else to compare it to.

EDWARD
I imagine it must feel very…directionless. To simply serve as a cog in a great device you cannot comprehend.

MIRIAM
I'm not certain that is how I feel.

EDWARD
Indeed?

MIRIAM
What I said before…I meant only that I am nothing compared to a king.

EDWARD
Yes, well, that's obvious, isn't it? Drink your wine.

MIRIAM
I do not drink, my lord.

EDWARD
And I do not request. Drink it.

(She does so)

EDWARD
Do you know what you were drinking to?

MIRIAM
I do not.

EDWARD
Peace, Miriam. You were drinking to peace. To the end of a war started before you were even born.

MIRIAM
It is a good thing to drink to.

EDWARD
Is it?

(A great crash of thunder. EDWARD turns to the window)

EDWARD
It has been years since I've seen a storm like this.

MIRIAM
I was told you inspected it first hand.

(He smiles a little)

EDWARD
I did indeed. It was…educational.

MIRIAM
Why did you do it?

(Beat)

MIRIAM
Forgive me. It is not my place to ask.

EDWARD
You care little for propriety. Am I correct?

MIRIAM
Yes, si...yes.

EDWARD
I can respect that. At times. I went out into the storm because it called to me.

(He sees she doesn't understand. He leads her to the window)

EDWARD
That sound you heard a moment ago. Lightning struck an old tree, blasted it in two. There. Do you know why it did that?

(She shakes her head no)

EDWARD
Because nature abhors peace as much as I do.

(He stares out the window, speaking to MIRIAM, but not looking at her)

EDWARD
For the past month, I have written no battle plans. I have sharpened no sword. I have led no men into the field. And every morning, I wake to the taste of dust in my mouth. The war with France is over, and I am old. I stare out at an England I do not recognize.

(He finally looks at MIRIAM)

EDWARD
Without an enemy, how do you define yourself?

MIRIAM
I wouldn't know.

(He laughs a bitter laugh, looks out the window)

EDWARD
You wouldn't know.

(He lays on the bed, looking upward)

EDWARD
When I was sixteen, I captured my first enemy in this very room.

MIRIAM
Your mother?

EDWARD
The usurper Roger Mortimer. You should have seen his face when he opened his eyes and saw me standing there, a dozen men at my back and my sword at his throat. It was glorious. I almost killed him then and there. But I didn't. Would you like to know why?

MIRIAM
If you wish to tell me.

EDWARD
I do! I do wish to tell you. I didn't kill him because…you must understand, Miriam, that this man had killed my father, and taken his kingdom. My mother had played her part, certainly, but Mortimer was the true villain here. But if I killed him then, Little Jew, he would not have suffered. I thought if I were to see him beaten down and disgraced, that I would feel some peace.

MIRIAM
Did you?

EDWARD
No. I felt bloodlust. The more Mortimer suffered, the more I wanted to see him suffer. It fed on itself until I finally had him hung, just to hear the sound of his neck breaking.

(He drinks)

EDWARD
I didn't kill the man because he took my rightful throne. No, I knew I would rule this kingdom in time. The real reason, Miriam…the real reason I killed the man was because he killed my father. Took him from my life. And for that, a thousand deaths would not satisfy me.

MIRIAM
Do you…regret it?

EDWARD
God, no. My only regret in killing him was that I couldn't raise him back to life and do it over again. There are no words to describe the joy I felt at seeing his corpse dancing in the gibbet.

MIRIAM
But you said you felt no peace.

EDWARD
That wasn't peace, child. No, that day I discovered something much stronger than peace…power. The power to see a wretched bastard endure every cruelty he'd earned in a lifetime of corruption. And I knew that peace would be a poor substitute for that.

(MIRIAM fights to control her disgust, and is only marginally successful)

MIRIAM
Do you even know what it means to be king?

(EDWARD sits up)

EDWARD
Now...that is an interesting question.

(He closes in on her. She backs into the wall, and he follows her)

EDWARD
Why do you run from me?

MIRIAM
You frighten me.

EDWARD
I don't believe you.

MIRIAM
Please, just...

EDWARD
When I looked into your eyes...what I saw there was not fear. You are not a rabbit, ready to jump in terror. No, there is some strength to you. Some... purpose.

MIRIAM
You do not know me.

EDWARD
Perhaps. Perhaps not.

(EDWARD walks away from her, and throws the window open. He savors the raging storm)

EDWARD
Tell me your thoughts on Pascal.

MIRIAM
What?

EDWARD
Pascal. The kindly French gentleman who brought you here.

MIRIAM
It is not my place to say.

EDWARD
It is your place to do as your king commands! Speak your thoughts or I shall beat them out of you!

(He slams the windows shut & stares at her)

MIRIAM
He is a good man.

EDWARD
What does that mean? A "good man"?

MIRIAM
He knows how to balance sternness with kindness.

EDWARD
Go on.

MIRIAM
He is a loyalist.

EDWARD
Is he?

MIRIAM
He spoke to me today about serving both your parents, and later you. I was left with the impression that he preferred you.

EDWARD
Do you speak often with Pascal? And so openly?

MIRIAM
He speaks to me. I listen.

EDWARD
Has he bedded you?

(She stops, full of outrage)

MIRIAM
Never.

EDWARD
Not once?

MIRIAM
Never.

EDWARD
Well, don't take it personally. It's likely just his age.

(He reads her expression)

EDWARD
That angers you?

MIRIAM
He is my friend.

EDWARD
So you are friends with your superior?

MIRIAM
He does not treat me that way.

EDWARD
How he treats you is irrelevant. He is your superior.

MIRIAM
Yes.

EDWARD
And you are friends?

MIRIAM
I...yes. It is permitted...

EDWARD
Of course it is. Simply a question. Here is another. Does he speak often of his home?

MIRIAM
This is his home.

EDWARD
France, girl. Does he speak often of France?

(Beat)

MIRIAM
Some. But not with any regularity.

EDWARD
Does he miss it?

MIRIAM
I don't think so. This is his home now.

EDWARD
It has been since I was a child. Do you know why he left France?

MIRIAM
He never told me.

(EDWARD smiles, unsure if he should tell her)

EDWARD
It's quite a tale. One that I shall let him share in

his time.

MIRIAM
Has he crossed you? Is that why you ask these questions?

(Beat)

EDWARD
One of the joys of being king is this- I may ask whatever questions I like, but I never have to answer.

MIRIAM
I simply meant...if you mean him ill, please hear me out. He is a kind man who lives to serve you. He...

EDWARD
You would take his part, even though you do not know if he has earned my ire?

MIRIAM
I would.

(Beat)

EDWARD
I may have misjudged you, Miriam, daughter of Saul. When I looked into your eyes before, do you know what I really saw?

MIRIAM
Strength. Purpose.

EDWARD
Blackness. A great, empty shadow staring through eyes too young to hold it.

MIRIAM
So you think I have no soul?

EDWARD
A few minutes ago, I might have thought that. But now...clearly, I need to reevaluate my opinion.

(He lies back down on his bed)

EDWARD
You are lovely.

(She responds with difficulty)

MIRIAM
Thank you.

EDWARD
If I were to ask you to join me in this bed, what would you say?

(Beat)

MIRIAM
I would say nothing. I would simply...join you.

EDWARD
You've made it clear that you see no wrong in befriending a superior. And with the possible exception of the Lord God himself, there is none superior to me.

MIRIAM
If you want me, why not just take me?

EDWARD
I never said I wanted you.

MIRIAM
You...but you called me lovely.

EDWARD
I never said I didn't want you either.

(He laughs)

EDWARD
You would have made a poor king, Little Jew.

MIRIAM
It's just as well. I could never grow a proper beard.

(He laughs even louder)

EDWARD
My god, you have a wit! I can see why the old dog has taken such a shine to you.

(She is about to respond. He silences her with a wave)

EDWARD
I meant no disrespect. Only that our dear Pascal clearly cares for you. Ah! There it is; our common ground!

MIRIAM
What?

EDWARD
Something we share...the affection of the King's Steward.

MIRIAM
Why do you seek common ground with me?

EDWARD
I told you before. I answer questions only if I choose to do so. Say too much, and you're giving your enemies a dagger.

MIRIAM
Are we enemies then?

EDWARD
That would be a strange thing.

MIRIAM
It almost sounds as though you fear me.

EDWARD
I have not felt fear in so long, I doubt I would even recognize it.

MIRIAM
One might think that a good quality for a king.

EDWARD
Perhaps.

(A long beat)

EDWARD
I am weary, Miriam.

MIRIAM
Shall I leave you to your slumber?

EDWARD
So anxious to escape me?

MIRIAM
Not at all.

EDWARD
And a terrible liar, too. I find myself wondering what your virtues are, beyond some semblance of beauty.

MIRIAM
I am a good cook.

EDWARD
I thought you were a scullery maid.

MIRIAM
I am both. With the loss of your other servants...

EDWARD
Yes, of course. You've taken on additional burdens. Did you make the Marchpane we dined upon this night?

MIRIAM
In fact, I did not. That was entirely Bess' doing.

EDWARD
Ah yes. Bess. Of course.

MIRIAM
From the look of the dining hall, it did not appear as though it was enjoyed.

EDWARD
I'm sure it was fine. But the storm beckoned me.

MIRIAM
The storm wished you to destroy the Marchpane?

EDWARD
It wished me to destroy something. And the cake was there.

(He drains his cup)

EDWARD
When the urge to wreak havoc rises, it can be too powerful to resist.

(He holds his cup out)

EDWARD
One more.

(She takes the goblet. She examines the bottle)

MIRIAM
There is not much wine left.

EDWARD
It has been a long night.

MIRIAM
Perhaps I...

EDWARD
Is there enough left for one final glass?

(Beat)

MIRIAM
Yes.

EDWARD
Then serve me.

(She faces the table in such a way that the King can only see her back. As they speak, she empties the ring into the cup, then fills it with wine)

EDWARD
I sometimes wonder if I slaughtered all those French pigs just for their wine.

MIRIAM
Hmm.

EDWARD
You're not French, are you?

MIRIAM
I am Jewish, your majesty.

EDWARD
Not to startle you, but there are Jews in France, Miriam.

MIRIAM
Of course.

EDWARD
It's a weak country. They try to win their battles with quills.

MIRIAM
Are you not descended from French royalty?

EDWARD
In fact I am. You're familiar with my lineage, then?

MIRIAM
Only that you used it as your claim to the French throne.

EDWARD
A good warrior utilizes any weapon in his arsenal.

MIRIAM
One might think that a single kingdom would be enough.

EDWARD
Is this world not God's kingdom? And am I not God's chosen servant?

MIRIAM
And again, we find common ground. We are both of us servants.

(Beat)

EDWARD
I cannot decide if I should be insulted or amused.

MIRIAM
It would be a strange thing for a cook to offend her king.

EDWARD
Most cooks do not possess your wit. It's incrementally charming.

MIRIAM
I'm certain his majesty will correct me if I overstep my bounds.

EDWARD
Few servants would risk my…correction.

MIRIAM
Since I am not French, perhaps I have a reserve of courage.

EDWARD
By night's end, we shall see.

(She turns around, cup in hand)

EDWARD
Come. Lie next to me.

(She stares at him, unmoving. For a moment, she's unsure she can go through with it)

EDWARD
Come.

(She walks to the bed & hands him the glass. She lies next to him. He does not attempt to be overly amorous. He smells the wine)

EDWARD
So here we have it. The dregs.

MIRIAM
It appeared to be a good vintage.

EDWARD
Even the best year reaches its final drop. I suppose there's a lesson in that.

MIRIAM
Perhaps at the end…

EDWARD
I know what the lesson is, Miriam.

(He puts his arm around her. Her body tenses. He holds the glass between them, staring at it)

EDWARD
My queen brought that bottle back with her, from a brief journey to France years ago. Before the war.

MIRIAM
I cannot help but wonder what she might think if she were to walk through those doors.

EDWARD
Philippa is in Scotland this night. We are quite alone.

MIRIAM
Do you love her?

EDWARD
I suppose it's possible.

MIRIAM
Then why am I here?

(He stares at her, then raises his glass a bit)

EDWARD
To unanswered questions.

(He brings the cup to his lips, watching MIRIAM at all times. He brings it to his mouth, but does not drink. Finally--)

EDWARD
You are the loveliest assassin I have ever known.

(Beat. EDWARD pours the wine on the floor. MIRIAM leaps from the bed and runs for the door.

EDWARD rises & hurls the goblet at the door. She recoils from the noise and backs directly into him. He snarls, and grabs her roughly)

EDWARD
You were right to fear me, little Jew.

(He grabs her throat in one hand, practically lifting her off the ground. He walks her to the window, opening it with his free hand. The storm rages outside. He pushes her towards the open window)

EDWARD
I could snap your neck. I could hurl you from this window and leave your broken carcass for my dogs. All this I could do, and none would call it murder. That is what it means to be king.

(She chokes out her words)

MIRIAM
Do it.

(He says nothing, just glares with fury)

MIRIAM
End...your lecturing...and do it.

(He raises his arm, seriously considering the possibility. Instead, he throws her roughly to the ground. She scrambles for the door)

EDWARD
There are four armed guards beyond that door.

(She turns, heading for another wall)

EDWARD
And another two in the secret tunnel.

(She freezes. He removes a dagger from beneath his pillow)

EDWARD
Of course I knew about it. How do you think I took Mortimer unawares?

MIRIAM
Rot in hell, you...!

(He grabs her again, throwing her to the bed. He points his dagger at her face)

EDWARD
I haven't spilled blood in weeks, child. And I am of a mind to scratch that itch.

MIRIAM
Then end it, you rank bastard. I fear neither death, nor you.

EDWARD
Perhaps not so quick an end. Perhaps an eye goes first, or an ear...perhaps I carve out your clever tongue.

MIRIAM
Look into my eyes again, king of nothing. You did not see fear then, nor will you see it now.

(He stares at her for a long time. He then releases her, sheathing his dagger. She scrambles away from him, but makes no escape. They just stare at each other for a while. Finally--)

MIRIAM
I live.

EDWARD
You do.

MIRIAM
Why haven't you killed me?

(He doesn't answer)

MIRIAM
Here I stand, an assassin in the King's chambers! Why do you not kill me?!

EDWARD
Perhaps because you want it so very much.

(He again goes to the window, looking out at the storm)

MIRIAM
You turn your back to me?

EDWARD
You're beaten and you know it.

MIRIAM
How did you know what I intended?

EDWARD
My spies linger in more places than foreign castles.

(Beat)

MIRIAM
Dulcie.

EDWARD
Not an impressive mind, but loyal.

MIRIAM
She told me you bed her.

EDWARD
And honest as well.

MIRIAM
You did all this just to entrap me?

(He smiles)

EDWARD
I bed her for no other reason than the desire to do so. You were caught because you were sloppy. I'm not in the habit of suspecting my servants, but she came to me while you and Pascal made your plans. Heard you through the door, apparently.

MIRIAM
I see.

EDWARD
Do you? Somehow I think not.

(He dons his robe)

MIRIAM
Do not ignore me!

(He goes to the window, ignoring her)

MIRIAM
You killed my father, you whoreson!

(Beat)

EDWARD
I've killed many times, in many lands, but I don't recall doing that.

MIRIAM
Yours might not have been the hand that did it, but you sent him to his death.

EDWARD
You are wrong, Miriam.

MIRIAM
You don't know, do you? You have no idea what happened to him.

EDWARD
I know enough.

MIRIAM
You know nothing! He was just another servant to you! Your "Little Jew" to be sent on this errand and that and to hell with the risk!

EDWARD
Yes, dammit! To hell with the risk! I cannot afford to wring my hands over the decisions I make!

MIRIAM
You sent him to Italy to die!

EDWARD
What in God's name are you talking about?

(She charges him. He grabs her by the arms and hurls her to the bed)

EDWARD
Be still!

MIRIAM
Do you know what they did to him? Did you even care to ask?

(He says nothing)

MIRIAM
He was captured by floggers. They forced him to sign a document, claiming he had come to Italy to poison the wells with the plague. He signed it because they told him they'd kill him otherwise. But zealots don't need to hold to their word.

(She stares at EDWARD, who clearly doesn't know what she means)

MIRIAM
The floggers used that paper as proof to what most believed already! The plague was God's curse on man, and the Jews were to blame. It wasn't enough that we'd been run out of almost every land, had virtually every freedom stripped from us. Now we were hunted and slaughtered like animals... because of my father's signature.

EDWARD
I cannot be blamed for that.

(She stands there, shocked)

EDWARD
I have kept the goddamn Flagellants out of my country. The Pope himself has denounced them. What happened to your father was unfortunate...

MIRIAM
Unfortunate?!

EDWARD
But my hands are clean.

MIRIAM
You knew he was a Jew, and still you sent him to a land where our kind is hated!

EDWARD
Where is your kind not hated?!

(Beat)

EDWARD
I bear no ill to your people. Nor have I ever. Your father knew that. It is why he petitioned me to join my servants. You should be thanking me that you live in the castle, where you can plot my death without Christian interference.

MIRIAM
You are a soulless bastard.

(Beat. These are the words that hit EDWARD hardest)

EDWARD
Yes, Miriam. I am.

(He goes to her, something cold rising inside him, like a threatening storm)

EDWARD
I fought this long war, and have felt nothing. I have taken a wife, sired twelve children...I have ruled this land for thirty years...and I have nothing to offer it but death.

(He removes his dagger)

EDWARD
I wonder...if I were to give you this, could you do it? Could you slide it between my ribs and pierce my heart? Or would the blade find nothing there but a great, dark hole.

MIRIAM
Give me the blade and I'll give you an answer.

EDWARD
It's a shame you were born a girl. You'd have made an excellent soldier.

MIRIAM
I have had years to turn myself into this, dreaming of the day when I would watch you sputter and die.

EDWARD
Because you think I had some hand in your

father's death?

MIRIAM
He should never have been sent away.

EDWARD
And Christ should have had one less guest for supper.

(He closes in on her)

EDWARD
You believe yourself a killer. You believe you have murdered all that was once human within you. Little girl, you cannot fathom what it is to take a life. I was younger than you when I first took one. And in all the years since then, I have become that which you seek to be.

(He looks at her for a while, then tosses the dagger at her feet. For a moment, she is uncertain. Then, she grabs it and goes for him. He bats her sloppy thrust away easily)

EDWARD
Pathetic. Worse than a novice.

MIRIAM
Bastard!

EDWARD
Where is your savagery? Where is your conviction?

(She cries out in rage, and manages to cut the King's hand. He recoils, then smiles darkly)

EDWARD
Yes. There it is. There is the beast behind your eyes.

(They circle each other, each trying to determine who will attack first)

EDWARD
Come for me.

(She does not)

EDWARD
A killer doesn't doubt, child. When the opportunity...

(She has circled to the small table. Before EDWARD can finish his thought, she hurls it at him. He bats it out of the way, momentarily leaving his back open to her. She pushes him over, then brings the dagger to his throat. He catches her hand before she can slit his neck, and she fights back)

EDWARD
Kill me and you'll die before you get five steps.

MIRIAM
I know. I've always known that.

(EDWARD manages to rise. He strikes MIRIAM hard in the face. She falls, and he retrieves her dagger)

EDWARD
I have a thought, child. Would you like to hear it?

(He kicks her in the stomach. She crumples to the ground)

EDWARD
It is my thinking that you wish for the peace of oblivion. Because your heart can no longer live with the truth. While your people died in Italy and Germany and Spain, you were here, safe, because of me.

(She charges again. This time he pins her to the bed)

EDWARD
You still remember what it was to love, to be loved. That part of you fights against the assassin. You cannot exist as both, so you seek release.

(He takes the dagger, holds it to her throat)

EDWARD
Tell me I am wrong. Tell me you wish to live, and I will let you walk from this room. Tell me that you do not wish me to draw this blade across your throat.

(Finally, MIRIAM's rage falters. She begins to weep)

MIRIAM
Kill me, you bastard. Do it!

EDWARD
I could do that. Yes. But I'm not done with you yet.

(He crosses to the door and leaves. She tries to cross away, but hasn't recovered from her beating. EDWARD quickly returns with a bruised & bloodied PASCAL. The King hurls him to the floor)

MIRIAM
No!

(MIRIAM goes to him)

EDWARD
Behold. The conspirators reunited.

PASCAL
Miriam...

(PASCAL reaches for her. EDWARD pulls her away)

EDWARD
No. There shall be no comfort.

MIRIAM
What have you done to him?

EDWARD
I've done nothing. My guards, however…can be a bit zealous.

(He drags PASCAL to a chair and throws him in it)

MIRIAM
Let him go!

EDWARD
No, Little Jew. There is only one freedom left for this traitor.

PASCAL
…my idea…all my doing…I confess…

EDWARD
And so you come to her aid?

PASCAL
…I drove her to this…she is innocent…

(The King laughs, then drags MIRIAM to PASCAL)

EDWARD
This is your innocent? This cur? Innocents do not poison their king.

(He shows PASCAL his bloody hand)

EDWARD
They do not draw blades against him either.

PASCAL
What do you want? I'll do anything...let her go...

MIRIAM
No!

EDWARD
So now, your nobility shows itself? Where was it when you decided to murder your oldest friend, hmm?

(EDWARD grabs PASCAL roughly. PASCAL cries out in pain)

MIRIAM
Stop. Please.

PASCAL
You killed them...you killed them all...

EDWARD
How's that?

PASCAL
My people...my countrymen...

EDWARD
Ah...here it is. This is why you sought to make me worm food?

(MIRIAM goes to him. EDWARD turns to her, dagger in hand)

EDWARD
Another step and I pierce his heart. I would hear Judas speak.

(MIRIAM backs off)

EDWARD
Henri...I have been killing the French most of my

life. Why now? What have I...?

PASCAL
...my sister... my sister, her children... Yvette, Guillaume, Murielle.... all dead.

(Beat)

PASCAL
...your soldiers burned Chalours to the ground... the entire village, gone. My friends, my family... none survived.

EDWARD
It was war, Henri!

PASCAL
They were innocents! Farmers, nothing more! You laid siege to a people who wanted nothing to do with your war, and left none alive! My God, Edward! I...I loved you, once. The bright, clever boy who became a man too soon. I stood by you then, because it was right to do so. But now...this is not peace, Edward. You know that.

EDWARD
That's not true.

PASCAL
I once believed you capable of leading us to something better, but now...

(EDWARD strikes PASCAL)

EDWARD
I've done what I've done for England!

MIRIAM
Leave him alone! I'm begging you!

EDWARD
I've brought prosperity to my people! Safety and strength and...

PASCAL
And you have nothing left.

(Beat)

PASCAL
When I took you in from the storm tonight, you said those very words to me. I didn't understand them...not at first. But now... You are no king, Edward. You're a sword that has killed and killed, and is now set upon a wall.

EDWARD
No, I...

PASCAL
Without war, you are nothing.

(A long beat)

EDWARD
And if I die while the peace still holds, then my son will claim the throne and keep the peace. Why, I wager you'd tell him it was my dying wish. How close am I to the mark?

(A long pause. EDWARD looks to MIRIAM)

EDWARD
He would have me killed to prevent another war. You would have me killed to avenge a death not of my making.

(He comes back to PASCAL)

EDWARD
Why her, Henri? Of all your friends, your allies...

why her?

MIRIAM
After you took my father from me, Pascal raised me. He knew he couldn't do the deed himself... and he knew I wouldn't falter.

(EDWARD smiles grimly)

EDWARD
Is that right?

(EDWARD tosses MIRIAM a cloth)

EDWARD
Clean the old wretch up.

(She goes to PASCAL, but keeps an eye on EDWARD)

EDWARD
I've known Pascal all my life. He showed me the hidden passages that allowed me to retake my throne as a boy. He never bloodies his own hands, but he's always willing to point killers towards their targets. Especially the motivated ones.

PASCAL
Edward, don't...

EDWARD
You've become too familiar with me, Steward. Call me "Edward" again, and I'll cut your tongue out.

PASCAL
If you would kill me, then...

EDWARD
One of you will die tonight. Perhaps both. But it only seems fair that you die knowing the truth.

(EDWARD closes in on MIRIAM)

EDWARD
It wasn't your need for revenge that Pascal sought, my dear. No, I think it was something else entirely. Something known to only him and me.

MIRIAM
He knows that I...

EDWARD
Yes, yes. The death of your father. But Pascal knows a secret about you, girl. Shall I tell it to you?

MIRIAM
What?

PASCAL
My lord, please...

EDWARD
No, the real reason he sent you to do me in...he knew the chances of success would be slim. So why not send an assassin that might cause the King to pause, to falter long enough to ensure his own demise? He hoped I would show you a measure of affection, and allow you to finish me off.

MIRIAM
That makes no sense.

PASCAL
Miriam, don't listen to him.

EDWARD
It makes perfect sense, if you know all the facts.

MIRIAM
Why would you show me any affection?

EDWARD
Why do you think?

(She says nothing, fearing the answer. EDWARD goes to the window, looks outside)

EDWARD
You were born early, yes? That's what they told you.

MIRIAM
I was born at seven months.

EDWARD
Yes. Seven months after your father laid with your mother. And nine months after I did.

(She backs away, on the edge)

MIRIAM
...no...

EDWARD
Oh yes. You are not my first by-blow, but you are the first I've told.

MIRIAM
No...that can't...

(She looks to PASCAL, who simply lowers his head)

EDWARD
There are many who would welcome this news.

(She collapses, her back against the wall. She's on the verge)

EDWARD
To think, all these years, it has been my blood in your veins.

MIRIAM
STOP! God, just...Stop!

(Beat. MIRIAM, despairing, goes to PASCAL)

MIRIAM
He's lying...tell me he's lying!

(PASCAL lowers his head. MIRIAM sits back, broken. EDWARD kneels to her)

EDWARD
You wished to be a killer, daughter? Then know this...so long as a single shred of love lives within you, then you are weak.

(She begins to weep)

EDWARD
There. Yes. You can feel it dying, can't you? Your last ember fades...

(She lunges at him, pounding on him, though he holds her off easily)

EDWARD
Now tell me which hurts worse...knowing that you're my child, or knowing that your dear Pascal has kept it from you all these years?

MIRIAM
How...how could you...?

PASCAL
You were a child...you loved Saul so much...I couldn't do it.

EDWARD
Yes, ever so noble. Especially when he meant for you to end my life.

PASCAL
I did it because I love you.

EDWARD
But remember, girl. He loved me once too. And still he set his dogs on me.

MIRIAM
Stop!

EDWARD
It makes one wonder what other secrets he's keeping.

(MIRIAM *grabs* PASCAL *roughly. He cries out in pain*)

MIRIAM
You raised me! You took me in and...all these years! You knew I was his all these years, and said nothing!

PASCAL
Miriam...

MIRIAM
I have lived with this hate for almost all of my life! You saw it, saw it killing me...and you let it grow. You let it turn me into...this!

PASCAL
I wanted you to remember your father.

MIRIAM
My father?! That vile, rutting, murderous thing is my father!

EDWARD
I have a thought.

MIRIAM
You betrayed me!

EDWARD
Then kill him.

(She turns to EDWARD)

EDWARD
I've decided to offer one of you a stay of execution. An attempt has been made on my life, true. But only one assassin need die tonight.

PASCAL
You sick animal.

EDWARD
I may be at that. Still, here is my offer. Take this knife, Miriam, and stab him through the heart. Do that, and you may walk out of my castle. I'll even set you up somewhere in England, where you'll be safe. By the sea, perhaps.

MIRIAM
No.

EDWARD
Then I kill you. I'll see one of you dead, and I do not care which.

MIRIAM
Why would you do this?

EDWARD
Because of all my children, you are the most like me.

(She stares at him, shocked)

EDWARD
My eldest will make a fine king, an excellent king.

But you and I...we have known what it is to be betrayed by those you love best. That is where murder lives, and you know it now.

(He offers her the dagger)

EDWARD
This blade is for the Frenchman. Make a move against me, and you'll be dead before you hit the ground.

PASCAL
Don't do this.

EDWARD
Quiet. No one cares what you have to say.

PASCAL
I love you.

EDWARD
And you've seen what his love is worth.

PASCAL
I shouldn't have lied to you. I know, but...

MIRIAM
But you did.

(She takes the dagger)

MIRIAM
I remember so clearly, Midwinter's Fest....I was no more than fifteen. The smells, the presents, the warmth...Henri, I remember the dress you had made for me. I loved you dearly then...and you loved me. That was the worst of your lies.

(She turns to PASCAL, walks behind him. She stares at EDWARD for a long time, then cuts PASCAL's bonds. He falls to the floor)

MIRIAM
I can't.

EDWARD
I'm sorry.

MIRIAM
There is a rightness to it. I know that. But...

EDWARD
Your heart still beats. More than mine ever has.

MIRIAM
You said only one of us dies tonight.

(EDWARD looks at her, laughs a bit)

EDWARD
My god, girl! You would really take his place at the executioner's block?

MIRIAM
I have been dead for a very long time, Edward. Tonight, it simply caught up to me.

(He drops PASCAL, goes to her)

EDWARD
I was wrong about you. There is steel in your soul, stronger than I could have guessed. I wish I had found such strength in my own children, rather than a scullery maid.

MIRIAM
I do not know how to keep living with this. I think a traitor's fate might be for the best.

(She goes to PASCAL, helping him up)

MIRIAM
Please, let me take him from this place. I don't

want him to see what comes next.

(EDWARD nods)

PASCAL
You...you saved me.

MIRIAM
Hush.

PASCAL
Thank you.

(She stares at him for a beat, then stabs the dagger deep into his back. He cries out as she twists the blade, then he falls to the ground, still. She collapses to her knees, panting)

EDWARD
Had he tried to stop you from taking his place, would you have killed him then?

MIRIAM
...help me...God help me...

(EDWARD takes a blanket, throws it over PASCAL's corpse)

EDWARD
The first life you take is the hardest.

MIRIAM
Stop talking.

EDWARD
Because you're not really killing your enemy. You're killing the most human part of yourself.

(She weeps)

EDWARD
The pain you feel...that part of you is dying. I

remember that pain well.

MIRIAM
After so many years?

EDWARD
Oh yes. And you will too. If you choose to live.

(Beat)

MIRIAM
You will let me live?

EDWARD
Yes.

MIRIAM
Why?

EDWARD
You were never my enemy. Nor was I yours.

MIRIAM
It's not that simple.

EDWARD
It is if I choose it to be.

(He helps her rise)

EDWARD
Miriam, there is no safer place for you than within these castle walls. I have no desire to throw you to the wolves.

MIRIAM
I can't return to the kitchens. I can't…Edward, I killed a man! I belong in the dungeons!

EDWARD
You aren't the first of my servants to take a life. And if the kitchens do not suit you any longer,

we'll find some place that does.

MIRIAM
How do I look Bess in the eye? Or Dulcie? Or any of them?

(He sits on the bed, then motions MIRIAM to do the same)

EDWARD
I wish I had an answer for you, child. This will be a hard thing for you to live with. As time passes, so the pain will fade. Oh, it will never disappear completely. But you will learn to let this go.

MIRIAM
I held on to my father's death for eight years.

EDWARD
Because Pascal wanted you to cling to that rage. You know that there is no point to that.

MIRIAM
Can you help me?

(He looks at her)

MIRIAM
Can you help me...forget?

EDWARD
No. But I can help you learn to live with it.

MIRIAM
Is that what it means to be king?

(He smiles)

EDWARD
It is, in fact.

(She rises)

MIRIAM
I...should I clean this up?

EDWARD
Send someone else to do it. Your night has been long enough.

MIRIAM
I'll return to my quarters then. By your leave.

EDWARD
You may go.

(She starts to leave)

EDWARD
Do you play chess?

MIRIAM
No. That is, I never learned.

EDWARD
I'll send for you tomorrow, and teach you. I feel you may have a knack for it.

(She smiles slightly, confused)

MIRIAM
All right. Good night, sire.

EDWARD
Good night, Little Jew.

(She leaves. EDWARD just stares at the window, listening to the rain. After a while, DULCIE enters)

DULCIE
M'lord?

(He turns to her, confused)

DULCIE
I...Miri told me to come in. To clean up. Said there was a mess.

(*He motions for her to come in. She sees PASCAL*)

DULCIE
Oh Christ! That's the steward!

EDWARD
Well, it was.

DULCIE
What happened?!

(*EDWARD stares at her. She immediately gets to cleaning*)

DULCIE
Beggin' your pardon. Not my place to...

EDWARD
He was a spy for France. And an assassin.

(*She looks at him*)

EDWARD
You were right to warn me, but your facts were... muddled.

DUCLIE
Please forgive me, I...

EDWARD
It's all right. In fact, Miriam was the one who saved me from him. Put a dagger in his back when he came for me.

DULCIE
Then I'm glad she was here, and that you're not hurt.

EDWARD
I'm simply...saddened. It appears the French have no intention of keeping to our newly-found peace. This cowardly attack proves it. I fear our only course may be...retaliation.

DULCIE
I was tellin' Bess "you can dream about peace, and you can dream about shitting gold, but the gold's more likely to happen first."

(Beat)

DULCIE
Forgive me. I speak when I shouldn't, and say nothin' when I...shouldn't.

EDWARD
Just clean, girl.

DULCIE
Oui, m'sieu...m'lord....yes.

(She cleans. EDWARD still stares out the window. Beat)

EDWARD
Girl?

DULCIE
Yes?

EDWARD
What sort of man am I?

DULCIE
A good one, m'lord. Real good one. Best I've ever known.

EDWARD
You needn't flatter me.

DULCIE
I'm not. You took me off the streets, gave me a nice job, put me in the castle. Life I'm livin' now....never would've dreamed I'd live it. Every day the rest of my life, I'm thanking God for you. And that's not flattery, m'lord. That's God's own truth.

(Beat)

EDWARD
I did all that?

DULCIE
Yes, m'lord.

EDWARD
Come here.

(She walks to him. He lifts her face to his, then kisses it once, gently. She begins to unbutton her blouse. EDWARD stops her)

EDWARD
No.

DULCIE
Oh. But I...

EDWARD
Not tonight.

(She stands there, unsure)

DULCIE
What am I to do then, m'lord?

EDWARD
Just stay here. Watch the storm with me.

(She goes to him. They both look out the window)

DULCIE
What are we lookin' at, m'lord?

EDWARD
The future.

(They both stare out again, briefly illuminated by the lightning. Lights fade)

END OF PLAY

ABOUT THE PLAYWRIGHT

Joseph Zettelmaier is a Michigan-based playwright and four-time nominee for the Steinberg/American Theatre Critics Association Award for best new play, first in 2006 for ALL CHILDISH THINGS, then in 2007 for LANGUAGE LESSONS, in 2010 for IT CAME FROM MARS and in 2012 for DEAD MAN'S SHOES. Other plays include SALVAGE, THE GRAVEDIGGER - A FRANKENSTEIN PLAY, NORTHERN AGGRESSION, DR. SEWARD'S DRACULA, INVASIVE SPECIES, THE SCULLERY MAID, NIGHT BLOOMING and EBENEZER.

POINT OF ORIGIN won Best Locally Created Script 2002 from the Ann Arbor News, and THE STILLNESS BETWEEN BREATHS also won Best New Play 2005 from the Oakland Press. THE STILLNESS BETWEEN BREATHS and IT

CAME FROM MARS were selected to appear in the National New Play Network's Festival of New Plays. He also co-authored Flyover, USA: Voices From Men of the Midwest at the Williamston Theatre (Winner of the 2009 Thespie Award for Best New Script). He also adapted CHRISTMAS CAROL'D for the Performance Network.

IT CAME FROM MARS was a recipient of 2009's Edgerton Foundation New American Play Award, and won Best New Script 2010 from the Lansing State Journal. His play DEAD MAN'S SHOES won the Edgerton Foundation New American Play Award in 2011.

Joseph is an Associate Artist at First Folio Shakespeare, an Artistic Ambassador to the National New Play Network, and an adjunct lecturer at Eastern Michigan University, where he teaches Dramatic Composition.

Available Plays by Joseph Zettelmaier

It Came From Mars

Ebeneezer - a Christmas Play

The Gravedigger
A FRANKENSTEIN PLAY
adapted from the novel by Mary Shelly

The Scullery Maid

For information about production rights, visit:
www.jzettelmaier.com

More Plays From SORDELET INK

A Tale of Two Cities
by Christoper M Walsh
adapted from the novel by Charles Dickens

The Count of Monte Cristo
by Christoper M Walsh
adapted from the novel by Alexandre Dumas

The Moonstone
by Robert Kauzlaric
adapted from the novel by Wilkie Collins

The Woman in White
by Robert Kauzlaric
adapted from the novel by Wilkie Collins

Season on the Line
by Shawn Pfautsch
adapted from Herman Melville's Moby-Dick

Hatfield & McCoy
by Shawn Pfautsch

Once A Ponzi Time
by Joe Foust

Eve of Ides
by David Blixt

Visit www.sordeletink.com for more!

NOVELS FROM
SORDELET INK

The Star-Cross'd Series
The Master Of Verona
Voice Of The Falconer
Fortune's Fool
The Prince's Doom
Varnish'd Faces & Other Short Stories

The Colossus Series
Colossus: Stone & Steel
Colossus: The Four Emperors

and coming 2015
Colossus: Wail of the Fallen

Her Majesty's Will
a novel of Wit & Kit

All by bestselling author David Blixt!
Visit www.sordeletink.com for more!

www.ingramcontent.com/pod-product-compliance
Lightning Source LLC
Chambersburg PA
CBHW071705040426
42446CB00011B/1916